THE TRINITY MISSION • RULE OF LIFE

THE WAY OF CHRIST

THE SIMPLE WAY • THE ANCIENT WAY
THE NARROW WAY

An Interpretation of the Rule of St. Benedict
For People with Jobs and Families
in the Modern World

PROLOGUE

Listen carefully, my brothers and sisters, to the teaching of those who have come before us and attend with the ear of your heart. Herein is a design for life, born in love; welcome it, and faithfully put it into practice. It is a Way of living gathered from the long obedience of men and women who preferred nothing to our Lord Jesus Christ, seeking first His kingdom and its righteousness. If you are willing, then give up your own way, as they did, for a way that is sure and good and tested by time.

Today, if you hear His voice, do not harden your heart as in the time of rebellion. But rather, come and listen, and learn the fear of the Lord our God, the only and one God; the God in whom we live and move and have our being as servants of Jesus, the Savior and Restorer of all things, who Himself is this God; the God who desires to build in each of us the still more excellent way.

Seeking laborers in a multitude of people, the Lord calls out to us saying: "Who among you desires life; who desires many days, that he may see good?" If, when you hear this, your hear leaps up, then God directs these words to you: "If you desire true and eternal life, keep your tongue from evil and your lips from speaking deceit. Turn away from evil and do good; seek peace and pursue it."

Once you have done this, the Lord says, "my eyes will be upon you and my ears will listen for your prayers; and even before you ask me, I will say to you: Here I am."

The voice of the Lord is calling to us continually. The Lord in His love shows us the way of life and good and blessing - and he calls us to walk in it. Clothed then with faith and the good works of God's people, let us set out on this Way, with the Gospel for our guide, that the eyes of our heart may be opened and we may see Him who has called us to be citizens of His glorious kingdom.

If we wish to dwell in this kingdom, we must determine to take action, to choose for ourself the way of life, for the Lord has told us who may dwell in His tabernacle and who may abide on His holy hill: "he who walks with integrity and does what is righteous and speaks truth in his heart; he who does not slander with his tongue and does no evil to his neighbor, nor casts slurs against his fellow man."

The contemplative life of the true disciple of Jesus is not only the hearing and reflecting on Holy Scripture but includes the living of it, embodying the word of God in the world. It is an incarnational life; one in which the word of Christ dwells richly in and among His people, to be witnessed and to bring glory to the Father.

God, through Christ, has gathered us and made us His people, a royal priesthood, a holy nation, that we may declare His praises and be a display of His glory. He has sent us into the world to make for Him disciples of all nations and to preach the good news of his kingdom to all creation. Therefore, since Christ is in us, guiding us and empowering us, let us also follow His example and move out to be His real and actual presence in the world.

Let us make a good plan, in order that we may live intentionally: in our work, our recreation, our rest, our time, our talents, our finances, and our relationships. Let us take captive every thought, every intention, every word, every action to make it obedient to Christ. Let us order our lives that He may serve the world through us and that we may understand more deeply that whenever and wherever we serve, it is Him whom we are serving.

Furthermore, we should always keep in mind that though He will equip us with everything good for doing His will and though He work in us what is pleasing to Him, the work and the glory are His. For everything under heaven belongs to God and there is no good we can do that the doing of which is not also a gift from God.

And so, here we shall establish a school for the Lord's service, a common design for our lives; setting down nothing harsh or burdensome, but only those things that make us more into the likeness of Christ; a contemplative, missionary, creative people; a people of prayer and Holy Scripture; laborers for the Lord, caretakers of His creation, participants in His work of reconciling all things to Himself in our Lord Jesus Christ; a people inspired, compelled, enabled, and directed by the Holy Spirit of Christ; a people who desire that in all things - thought, word, and deed - and that in all parts of the culture and the creation we might bring glory to the Name of Christ giving thanks to the Father through Him. For this purpose, we order our lives according to this design, each in accordance with his particular gifts and station of life, that we may be available and faithful to the Holy Spirit's guidance and creativity.

The way that we describe here is a way that is good, trustworthy, and a historical way of being a Christian; a way that exemplifies the faith once delivered to the saints. It is a way that is rooted in the Rule of Benedict as it has developed in the Anglican prayer-book tradition.

But let us maintain all humility in this endeavor, recognizing that this is not the only good way of following Christ. Each of us must be fully convinced in our own mind so that as we live, we live to the Lord, and when we die, we die to the Lord, for we are the Lord's.

Finally, let us rebuke every hint that we preach ourselves or this design for living, for our message is that Jesus Christ is Lord and we are His servants. Rather, all who follow this Way must seek to have the mind of John the Baptist who found his joy made complete in the incarnation of Christ when he stated, "He must become greater; I must become less."

So, my dear brothers and sisters, let us gather together, that we may be true to our calling and let us order and cultivate our lives in a manner that is trustworthy and consistent with the faith and practice of the followers of Christ throughout history and around the world so that the Spirit of Christ may work through us as He forms His people to be a display of His splendor, a blessing for all the earth. Come now, let us taste and see the goodness of the Lord in the land of the living.

HE GOOD WAY

There are various ways of following Christ, some are better than others. First, there are those Christians who constrain their beliefs by the consensus of the Church's teaching through two-thousand years; who order their lives as the followers of Christ have done since the days of the Apostles; who worship in spirit and in truth as the Church has done since Pentecost; in short, those who align themselves with the Great Tradition of Christian belief and practice.

Secondly, there are those Christians who mistakenly believe that the teaching or practice they have personally experienced in their short and geographically limited lives is in fact the Great Tradition of two-thousand years. These believers are to be commended for looking outside of themselves to learn the faith and for their willing-ness to receive a faith delivered to them by their elders. But sadly, their experience may be only of a tradition that is merely five, fifty, or five hundred years old and not the faith as it was handed down from the time of the Apostles. For these brothers and sisters, much of what we are about to say may likely be foreign or confusing.

Third, are those Christians who ignore or even demonize the trea-sury of thought and the unbroken chain of practices delivered to us through the two-thousand years of men and women around the world who have followed Jesus as their Lord. Like a child lost in the woods, these Christians must rediscover in every generation and for each individual what life in Christ should look like. They become their own personal Pope and are ironically dumbfounded when their converts reject their own teaching. They do not look for an authority greater than their own personal opinion. For them, this Way may have little to offer.

Fourth and finally, are those who do not actually follow Christ at all but only apply His Name to themselves and their thinking while knowing nothing of Him in prayer and the Scriptures; those who do not have the integrity of the rich young ruler to simply walk away; who are unwilling to be like Peter and the Apostles and leave everything and follow Him.

Let us proceed to draw up a plan for the first kind, those who ask for the ancient paths, who look for the good way. It is for such as these that we embark on our singular goal:

TO DESCRIBE CLEARLY A WAY OF FOLLOWING CHRIST THAT IS CONSISTENT WITH CHRISTIAN PRACTICE THROUGHOUT HISTORY AND AROUND THE WORLD AND THAT IS ACHIEVABLE IN OUR OWN DAY BY MEN AND WOMEN WITH JOBS, FAMILIES, AND OTHER DAY~TO~DAY OBLIGATIONS.

It is important to remember that what we describe here is not a righteous requirement but simply an authentically Christian way of living. Some may adhere to this Way more closely and some more loosely. As beginners, we should not expect to attain to the whole life of this Way in a short time. It is a journey that will ever call us further up and further in.

BEGINNING THE JOURNEY

Historically, this design, this Way, would be called a "rule of life," by which we mean only that it is a good and right way by which we *wish* to order our lives. It is a well thought out, general description of how we *want* to live our life to the glory of Jesus Christ. It is a tool by which we might measure our progress; a goal which we aim to achieve. The point of a rule of life is to chart a course onward and upward into the knowledge and experience of God's grace, to describe what we want our life to look like and to describe it realistically, so that we might begin to attain to it.

As infants, we are carried along by a mother or father or someone else who loves us and is able to care for us. Those of us who are healthy then proceed to crawl, to walk, to run and dance and to carry children in our own arms. Should a gradual development with the help of others not be the same in our life in Christ?

This is a Way for beginners in the life of prayer, which we will find on the last day that we all are. Be neither too gentle nor too harsh with yourself as you proceed. Find for yourself a mother or father who has walked in this way longer than you have; someone who can encourage you and caution you so that you may not fall into slothfulness nor faint from the exhaustion of too great a zeal.

Great care should be taken in seeking out this person to walk with you and guide you, who will listen to the Spirit of Christ with you. Choose for yourself someone who can point out that which is good, right, and true at least as much by their example as by their words.

This pathway is a long journey and it bears repeating: do not expect to achieve the whole of this Way in a short time. Take one step today and one step only. Take another step tomorrow. When you have taken a step without Christ, stop and turn around. When you fall, look for the Lord and get back up. If you cannot, then simply call on the Lord and wait. In everything, pray before beginning, pray while doing, pray when done. What is not possible for us to achieve by nature, let us ask the Lord to supply by the help of his grace.

THE KIND OF PEOPLE WE ARE TO BE

It is for freedom that Christ has set us free. Let us stand firm so that we are not burdened once again by a yoke of slavery. Let us live by the Spirit as we grow in grace as Christ's disciples. Our lives then should be marked by the cultivation of the following tools of the spiritual craft:

To love the Lord God with all of our heart, mind, soul, and strength
To love our neighbor as our self
To honor all people equally
Not to do to another that which we would not want done to ourselves
To act differently from the world's way
To consider others as more important than our selves
To deny one's self that we may live to follow Christ
To relieve the poor and oppressed
To visit the sick
To show compassion on those in prison
To offer help in time of need
To console the sorrowful
To love outsiders well and appropriately
To offer Godly hospitality
To prefer nothing to the love of Christ
Not to give way to anger
Not to foster a desire for revenge
Not to entertain deceit in the heart
To do no evil by action or inaction
To be a person of integrity
To do no injury and to bear patiently injury done to us
To endure persecution for the sake of righteousness
To love our enemies

To pray for our enemies
To actively pursue goodness and good works
Not to be proud but
To acknowledge the presence of one's gifts and
To glorify God by recognizing them truly as gifts
Likewise, to acknowledge the evil we commit as our own and
To confess our sin readily
To continually seek repentance unto Christ
To keep our future death daily before our eyes
To keep watch over all that we do
Not to be given to drunkenness or gluttony
Not to be lazy
Not to be a murmurer or gossip
Not to be quarrelers
To guard against wicked or malicious speaking
To always trust in God
To exemplify freedom and abundant life in Christ
To apply ourselves often to prayer
Not to aspire to be called holy before we have become so
To live by God's commandments
To harbor neither hatred nor jealousy of anyone
To do nothing out of envy or selfish ambition
To shun arrogance
To be exemplary in all relationships
To work restoratively
To be cultivators
To be stewards after God's own heart
To pursue excellence in all things
To be sexually pure
To honor the aged
To love and respect the younger
To seek peace
To glorify God in thought, word, and deed
And finally, to never lose hope in God's mercy

Our daily lives of home, family, work, friendships, and our many other obligations will be the workshop where we shall toil faithfully at all these tasks. Therefore, let us now proceed to describe what this life in Christ shall look like.

THE BOUNDARIES OF OUR BELIEFS & PRACTICE

We who follow this Way claim to have "no peculiar thought, practice, creed or confession of our own but only the Catholic Faith of the ancient Catholic Church, as preserved in the Catholic Creeds and maintained in the Catholic and Apostolic constitution of Christ's Church from the beginning. We may licitly teach as necessary for salvation nothing but what is read in the Holy Scriptures as God's Word written or may be proved thereby. We therefore embrace and affirm such teachings of the ancient Fathers and Councils of the Church as are agreeable to the Scriptures, and thus to be counted apostolic. The Church has no authority to innovate: it is obliged continually, and particularly in times of renewal or reformation, to return to 'the faith once delivered to the saints.'" (*Archbishop Geoffrey Fisher speaking about the Anglican Communion*)

To the above, we make the following clarifications:

We confess the canonical books of the Old and New Testaments to be the inspired Word of God, containing all things necessary for salvation, and to be the final authority and unchangeable standard for Christian faith and life.

We confess Baptism and the Supper of the Lord to be Sacraments ordained by Christ Himself in the Gospel, and thus to be ministered with unfailing use of His words of institution and of the elements ordained by Him.

We confess the godly historic Episcopate (Bishops) as an inherent part of the apostolic faith and practice, and therefore as integral to the fullness and unity of the Body of Christ.

We confess as proved by most certain warrants of Holy Scripture the historic faith of the undivided church as declared in the Symbol of Faith, also called the Nicene Creed, which follows:

We believe in one God,
the Father, the Almighty,
maker of heaven and earth,
of all that is, visible and invisible.

We believe in one Lord, Jesus Christ,
the only-begotten Son of God,
eternally begotten of the Father,
God from God, Light from Light,
true God from true God,
begotten, not made,
of one Being with the Father;
through him all things were made.
For us and for our salvation he came down from heaven,
was incarnate from the Holy Spirit and the Virgin Mary,
and was made man.
For our sake he was crucified under Pontius Pilate;
he suffered death and was buried.
On the third day he rose again in accordance with the Scriptures;
he ascended into heaven
and is seated at the right hand of the Father.
He will come again in glory to judge the living and the dead,
and his kingdom will have no end.

We believe in the Holy Spirit, the Lord, the giver of life,
who proceeds from the Father,

who with the Father and the Son is worshiped and glorified,
who has spoken through the prophets.
We believe in one holy catholic and apostolic Church.
We acknowledge one Baptism for the forgiveness of sins.
We look for the resurrection of the dead,
and the life of the world to come. Amen.

In those things which are not clear from Holy Scripture in their
canonical sense, we will seek out the teaching and practice of the
Church, East and West, throughout history going back to the time
of the Apostles, and where we find greater consensus, we will hold
more firmly and where we find great variability, we will allow the
same.

TIMES OF PRAYER

From ancient times, God's people have had a practice of setting
apart certain times of the day for formal prayer and meditation in
God's word. It is desirable that we should maintain this habit in our
own lives, setting apart a specific time in the morning and in the
evening to come before the Lord in formal prayer.

In addition to these times of Morning and Evening prayer, it is good
to have other moments throughout the day at which we turn our
thoughts formally to the Lord, but these times will be more variable
according to our various circumstances.

Each household and individual will have to determine what is prop-
er and attainable in their situation - both regarding the number of
formal prayer tines and the manner of those times. It can be helpful
to remember two things here: one, routine is the basic course that
allows for creativity - and two, intimacy can be obscured by formal-

ity. Our formal times of prayer should be done in a way that shows reverence and intention but that is natural to the setting.

It is also suggested that our private (individual) prayers, including the reading of Holy Scripture, should be spoken aloud even if only a whisper.

Following, we shall provide some guidelines for developing an order of prayer in our lives.

*M*ORNING PRAYER

Morning Prayer should usually be prayed within an hour or so of waking. Any Benedictine, Anglican, or similar structure can be used but the full and regular form ideally should include at least one psalm, at least one other selection of Holy Scripture, the Lord's prayer, and intercessions for the whole Church, the ministers of the Church, the government of the local nation, and the poor and other vulnerable in the local community.

In many households, Morning Prayer will only be said privately (individually). But where the parents or the household prefers, it is good to say it corporately (gathered together) as well. Where Morning Prayer is said both privately and corporately, a shorter form may be used for one of the times of prayer.

The regular practice of Morning Prayer should be considered a foundational habit of the daily life of people who follow this Way.

EVENING PRAYER

An intentional moment of Evening Prayer is a second foundational prayer habit.

Evening Prayer should be prayed at some time after the majority of the day's work (minus perhaps some household chores) has been completed. In some households this may be just before supper, just after supper, or some time before bed. The liturgical form of the Evening Prayer office or the form of Compline may be used or adapted as necessary for the household. At a minimum, Evening Prayer should consist of the Lord's prayer followed by thanksgivings and other petitions.

At the time of Evening Prayer or at some other time of the evening, we would recommend taking a moment to reflect with the Lord upon our day; to notice where he has been at work; to notice where we have failed; to notice where he has been faithful; to notice our successes; and to receive whatever benefit from the day that we may take with us into the next day.

FAMILY PRAYER

Members of a family living in the same household ideally should gather together every day for at least Morning or Evening Prayer if not both. In families with full activity schedules, we suggest that life should be ordered so that the daily time of family prayer is the norm (four times a week or more) even if it does not occur every day.

The structure of family prayer time naturally will evolve as family size and age of children change. Parents will benefit from our resource *Getting Started with the Daily Office in the Household.*

$\mathcal{M}$ID-DAY PRAYER AND COMPLINE

As each person's life situation allows, there is much benefit to having an extended moment of prayer at mid-day and at bedtime as well. When circumstances allow, you may wish to make use of the full form of these services found in our community's daily prayer book or in many other Benedictine or Anglican resources. At other times, a brief recollection may be used. Examples of a brief recollection are provided in our resource *Getting Started with the Daily Office in the Household.*

$\mathcal{M}$EALTIME PRAYER

Just as it was the habit of our Lord to give thanks over his food and drink, we too should not neglect a prayer at mealtime. It is recommended that at meals, everyone at the table should be invited to join in the response from Psalm 145 below and then the head of the household or some other person appointed shall say the following grace (or some other way of making the same acknowledgements).

We use the "†" symbol to mark where it is customary to make the sign of the Cross.

Everyone (Psalm 145:15-16)
The eyes of all look to you,
and you give them their food in due season.
You open your hand
and satisfy the desire of every living thing.

Leader
Blessed are you O Lord our God, Creator, and King, for the
earth is yours and all that it brings forth and you have given to
us abundantly; we thank you for (*this food, family, friends, etc.*);
make us to be truly grateful for these gifts we have received,
and ever mindful of the needs of others, in the Name of the †
Father, and of the Son, and of the Holy Spirit. Amen.

A brief prayer, such as the following, may be said when alone or
when the situation calls for brevity.

† In the Name of the Father, and of the Son, and of the Holy
Spirit. Amen.

Bless us, O Lord. and these Your gifts, which we are about to
receive from Your bounty, through Christ our Lord. Amen. †

It is also suggested that a short thanksgiving, such as what follows,
be said at the conclusion of the meal.

Leader or Everyone Together
†In the Name of the Father, and of the Son, and of the Holy
Spirit. Amen.

We thank you, Lord, for this meal and for all your many mer-
cies; blessed be your Name, now and forever. Amen. †

PRAYER AT OTHER TIMES

The word of God is a lamp to our feet and a light to our path and yet we are exceedingly afflicted by the world, the flesh, and the devil. That we may be revived; that we may be washed and renewed; that we may train ourselves to pray without ceasing, we have found it beneficial to have a thought from Holy Scripture and other prayers to be used at anticipated regular moments of the day. Some examples follow. Others may be drawn from various prayer books and similar resources or from your own reading of God's word and responding to that upon which he may desire for you to meditate.

Upon Rising from Bed (Psalm 25:1-2)
† To you, O Lord, I lift up my soul. O my God, in you I trust. Glory be to the …

When Leaving the House (Psalm 121:8)
† May the LORD watch over my (our) going out and my (our) coming in from this time forth, and forevermore. Glory be to the …

Bedtime Prayers (Psalm 4:8 & Compline)
I will lay me down and sleep in peace; for you alone, O LORD, make me to dwell in safety. Amen. †

   ---then---

Guide us waking, O Lord, and guard us sleeping, that awake we may watch with Christ, and asleep we may rest in peace. Amen. †

   ---then---

Almighty and Merciful Lord grant us a quiet night, and at the last a perfect end; and the blessing of God Almighty, † the Father, the Son, and the Holy Spirit, be upon us and remain with us this night, and for evermore. Amen.

Bedtime Prayer for Children - The following may be added before or in place of the "I will lay me down" prayer from Psalm 4 in the above Bedtime Prayers
Now I lay me down to sleep. I pray the Lord my soul to keep. Your love be with me through the night and wake me with the morning light. Amen. †

Prayers for Any Time

A Prayer of the Desert Fathers Commonly Known as The Jesus Prayer
Lord Jesus Christ, Son of God, have mercy on me, a sinner.

Drawn from the Psalms and also recommended by the Desert Fathers
O God, make speed to save me. O Lord, make haste to help me.

Hearing the Word of God

Everyone should find achievable ways of hearing the word of God daily by reading, listening, or both. For those just reading the Bible through for the first few times, it will be helpful to have a guide, either a book or a person, to help you with understanding what you are reading.

Each of us should establish a plan for hearing the greater part of Holy Scripture on a regular basis in our life. If not using a suitable daily lectionary (reading plan) for Morning and/or Evening Prayer, then a plan should be created that achieves at least the following:

- Reading the whole New Testament, Psalms, and Proverbs at least yearly
- Reading Genesis, Exodus, Deuteronomy, Isaiah, and Jeremiah at least every two years
- Reading the remainder of Scripture as often as is possible in your life

In addition to a general reading plan, it is good to always have a short passage of Holy Scripture that we are working to commit to memory.

WEEKLY WORSHIP AND HOLY COMMUNION

To be a eucharistic people, that is, a grateful and joyful people, is to receive all things as a gift from God and to offer them back to God with thanksgiving. The central and initial place that we do that is in participating in the Son of God's offering of Himself for the life of the world by receiving Him in the bread and wine of Holy Communion. This has always been the primary distinguishing element of Christian worship.

Everyone should participate in some form of weekly gathered worship, preferably on the Lord's Day, as that has been the regular day of Christian worship throughout history.

For many of us, the local Christian community with which we may worship regularly may not hold the historical and sacramental understanding of Holy Communion – that means, at least, that we, by participating in Christ's perfect offering of Himself, are offering all of ourselves to God and receiving back from Him the lifegiving body and blood of Christ in the consecrated bread and wine.

In those places where the local, regular, weekly worship service does not express the historical, sacramental understanding of Holy Communion, you should seek to find for yourself (and your family) some other church body where you can receive the Eucharist as frequently as possible – ideally, once a month at minimum. A traveling distance of one hour should not be considered too far to achieve this.

Catholic Apostolic Teaching

We shall endeavor, each as befits their ability, to seek out catholic apostolic teachers from whom we may learn. Hopefully, this will come from the pulpit of our own parish. But in addition to this, or where this option does not exist locally, it may come from the reading of the writings of the early church or the reading or listening to podcasts of modern day catholic apostolic teachers.

When we say "catholic apostolic teaching" we mean that which is consistent with Holy Scripture as it has been understood in the Church throughout history and around the world. A teaching or practice that was or has been done only for a season or only in some part of the world is not "catholic." Likewise, a thought or practice, no matter how widely it has been accepted, that is not consistent with the plain teaching of Holy Scripture is not "apostolic."

Let us stand apart from new expressions, or new understandings, or re-imaginings of the Christian faith or of Jesus Christ our Lord and instead seek out the faith once delivered to the saints.

FASTING

Fasting is a gift from the Lord and a tool for building spiritual strength. It is not a legal requirement. However, our Lord did assume his disciples would fast when he gave them instructions on how to fast by saying, "*when* you fast."

Being careful not to establish a "law" of fasting or a cause for spiritual elitism, we shall now proceed to outline a fasting practice that is consistent with the practice of the earliest days of the Church. Each person shall prayerfully apply this practice to their own life making necessary adjustments and accommodations in accordance with their own situation and personal health.

Depending on the context and the length of the fast, a fast will generally consist of either eating nothing at all or of abstaining from meat, sweets, alcohol (except in the Holy Communion), and savory foods. For those who, for health or other reasons, are unable to fast from *all* food, it is perfectly acceptable to determine a "full fast" of a simple diet that maintains both the spirit of a fast and personal safety. Furthermore, the sick, the pregnant, the very young, and the very old have generally been exempt from fasting practices.

The oldest weekly fasting practice of the Church, and the one we recommend, is to fast on all Wednesdays and Fridays of the year except during Christmastide and Eastertide. Over time, in the West, this became a Friday-only fast and then a Fridays-in-Lent-only fast. But we recommend a return to the old way.

During a Wednesday and Friday fast, it is suggested that nothing shall be eaten at all (a full fast) from waking until at least after the noonday hour. It may be noted that in the past, this fast would generally last until the 9th hour of the day, 3:00pm. If family or business obligations do not allow for a full fast, perhaps abstaining from particular foods or some other equivalent practice can be attempted with the goal of maintaining the spirit of a fast on these days.

The other Holy Day fasts we recommend are as follows:

- On Ash Wednesday: a full fast from waking until after sunset (though we may receive Holy Communion).

- During Holy Week, from sunset on Palm Sunday until after the Easter Vigil: a fast from all meat, sweets, alcohol (except for Holy Communion), and savory foods.

- On Good Friday: a full fast from waking until after sunset (we may receive Holy Communion).

- On Holy Saturday: a full fast from waking until the Easter Vigil.

Also, it is customary to make some sort of intention during the whole of Lent. Likewise, there are other times throughout the year and in the life of a Christian when it may be appropriate to fast. Local custom and the guidance of a spiritual mother or father should be sought out in determining other times of fasting as needed for re-ordering our dis-ordered affections.

CONFESSION AND RECONCILIATION

In addition to the daily habit of self-examination and confession in the Offices and the weekly practice of confession at the Eucharist, no less than once a year, we shall each extensively examine ourselves and our lives and make a private confession to another person, ideally a priest/presbyter. For help with this, see our resource, *Making a Good Confession*.

$\mathcal{A}$LMSDEEDS

As followers of Christ, we shall, each one, continually strive more and more to do, to work for, and to act for justice; to love mercy and kindness; and to walk more humbly with the Lord our God. We are to be marked by our service to and walking with the poor, the parentless, the elderly, the immigrant, the homeless, the sick in body and mind, the lonely, the imprisoned, and the persecuted.

It is the responsibility of each one individually to find ways for themselves to participate regularly and helpfully in such work in their local area. When performing almsdeeds, we should keep in mind that our work is not about accomplishments but, rather, it is about acting with love and mercy toward our neighbor and in obedience to our Savior.

$\mathcal{G}$ENEROSITY AND GIVING

The tithe, or ten percent of our increase, has been the traditional target for Christian giving to the Church and certainly some portion of our finances should be given to our local congregation. This is done as an act of obedience to our Lord and is not based upon the administrative abilities of the parish. Those who earn more may choose to give more while those in financial hardship may need to give less for a time, as needed, to re-stabilize their situation.

In addition to whatever we tithe to our church, freewill offerings should be made to people, ministries, and other organizations as we are able. Those who live according to this Way shall be a people of abundant generosity. Giving with a cheerful heart and in such a way that our left hand does not know what our right hand is doing. In modern terms that will mean, at least, that not all of our giving is accounted for on tax returns.

Economic disparity shall grieve us and we shall eschew every notion that any economic advantage we have or may gain over another is due to our own work or ingenuity remembering that there is no such thing as a "self-made man," but only arrogant and ungrateful men with bad memories.

The earth is the Lord's and all that is in it. Let us remember this in our attitudes and actions regarding all things that have been placed in our custody or possession so that we might administrate those things, which are God's, in accordance with God's heart and with His values.

Hospitality

The Scriptures reveal that some of those who cross our paths are in fact angels. St. Benedict encourages us to treat every person who comes into our life as if he or she was Jesus Christ himself, for it is Christ who will one day say: I was a stranger and you welcomed me.

We too should be a people of great hospitality, first making Christ welcome in our home and then welcoming all others as we have welcomed Christ. For whoever does not love his neighbor whom he sees, cannot love God whom he has not seen.

We practice this Godly hospitality by actively and cordially welcoming others into our lives and spaces; by being attentive to the needs and experience of others; by being generous with our time, possessions, and abilities; by being thoughtful in word and deed; and by being kind, friendly, patient, and loving in the face of inconvenience.

Home Life

Our private lives should be ordered and lived as a people aware that we live in the sight of God. The question "is this good, profitable, and/or pleasing to the Lord" is a helpful tool of discernment for evaluating the way we treat the members of our household; the books, magazines, movies, and other media we consume; the way we order our finances; and the way we spend our "free time."

Simplicity

Regarding the things of this world, let us choose simplicity over extravagance asking, "can I do with less" rather than, "can I get more;" "is the one I have sufficient" rather than, "can I get a new one."

t Work

In the beginning, God put us into the garden to work and to care for his creation. We should be a people who work diligently in all our endeavors as though working for the Lord, that we might provide for ourselves and have an abundance to share with those in need.

We should be quick to serve as Christ came to serve; to lead by serving; and to follow without grumbling.

For those who own businesses, we should be exemplary in the pay rates of our employees and treat them well and with great compassion. We should be known in our community to be of the highest integrity in all business dealings.

Caring for God's Creation

The earth is neither a resource for our own self-pleasure nor a resource borrowed from the future. The earth is the Lord's. We do not treat the creation (plants, animals, soil, water, air, etc.) with greed, contempt, or self-indulgence. Neither do we deify it.

The creation is the work of the Lord's hand and it may be and must be used in accordance with His values and in a way that is honorable to Him. We should be known in our various communities as a people who care about God's creation. And we should treat the creation with honor and dignity consistent with its being the possession of the King who made it and shares it with us.

EING CREATIVE

By the word of the Lord all things are made; as He speaks things come into being and thus all of creation is a communication. From the beginning, God has allowed us to participate in His speaking of the creative word, in His naming and giving meaning and right order. As Christ restores us to our original intents and purposes as God's people, we can once again speak creative words into the world, words that form and shape, that proclaim who or what a thing truly is, words that communicate, that reveal, that provide a context for others to participate in their own understanding that they might understand from their own perspective.

For those of us who are artists or craftsman, let us work to be a Godly creative presence in this world, to be revealers of the truth in Christ through form and function. Let us speak creative words into this world, words of sound, light, shape, thought, order, movement, meaning, and purpose. And in every sphere where this is done, we should strive for excellence unwilling to exchange the glory of the immortal God for popularity or fortune. Let us seek God as the supreme master of our craft, for it is He who reveals Himself in all that has been created.

CULTIVATING STILLNESS BEFORE GOD

Beginning from our own personal disposition and not from another, we should each work to cultivate stillness in our life that we may become increasingly capable of hearing the voice of the Lord. The initial steps of this are achieved by setting a regular time during which we eliminate all electrical devices and appliances and either sit - or walk at a pace far slower than our usual pace.

One day of our week should be set aside for rest and restoration of our bodies, minds, and spirits. This may be the historical sabbath of Saturday, or Sunday - the Lord's Day - or some other day if the work schedule so requires.

In addition to a daily practice of stillness and silence, and a weekly sabbath rest, it will also be found to be of great benefit for each of us to have regular occasions each year of more prolonged quiet solitude with the Lord.

Annual Retreat

It is desirable that we take a number of days annually in a time of retreat for prayer and prayerful reflection upon our life and our living according to this Way.

A More Specific Elaboration Made by Each One

Each of us should write our own personal chapter elaborating on this Way and applying it more specifically to our self and our own circumstances. Furthermore, this personal chapter should be re-assessed at least annually so that this Way itself does not become an idol or avenue for ignoring the voice of the Holy Spirit.

See Appendix A, *Creating a Rule for Yourself and Your Family*.

$\mathcal{O}$N Accountability

Let us seek to encourage one another so that we may not be hardened by sin's deceitfulness and thus turn away from the living God. To this effect, we shall each take measures to hold ourselves accountable by other people primarily to the profession of being a disciple of Christ and secondarily to the lifestyle adopted by following this Way. This exercise shall be conducted in such manner that it is legitimate and useful. Great care should be taken so that its importance is not relegated to the level of meaningless or tedious action.

$\mathcal{C}$ONCLUSION AND MODIFICATION

Herein lies the design for our lives, a little rule that has been written for beginners yet sufficient for the more mature. It would be a great misunderstanding of the spirit of this Way to treat it as "rules," or regulations, or requirements one must meet in order to earn God's favor, for it is in God's love that we live and move and have our very being. We cannot earn that which has already been freely given.

Following Christ is about union with God and this Way we have described is a tool in that pursuit. It is not a way to manipulate the Holy Spirit, who comes and goes as he pleases, nor is it a way to achieve holiness by our own efforts. Following Christ and allowing the Holy Spirit to form Christ in us is a lived experience that cannot be confined to an organized system. What we have described here is a historical manner of tending the soil of our souls that we might better receive the seed of God's Word and His Kingdom; it is a way of life passed on from the times of the Apostles.

This Way seeks only to describe clearly a good and tested way of ordering our lives that we may draw closer to our God - Father, Son, and Holy Spirit; that we might stand firm in one spirit with the generations of Christians who have come before us; that we may contend as one body for the faith of the gospel of Jesus Christ; that we may conduct ourselves in a manner worthy of Christ's disciples; and that the Holy Spirit of Christ may find a welcome home in our hearts.

It may be amended from time to time as we seek to give a clearer expression of how one may follow Christ according to this way. We desire that it contain nothing novel or extreme but, rather, simply expresses an ancient way of living as a Christian that can be lived out in our own day.

My brother, my sister, do not ask yourself, "am I living this way already" or even, "can I live this way fully today," but first ask, "is this way good, right, and true," and then ask, "with God's help, am I willing to take a single step along this way today?"

*A*DOPTING THIS RULE FOR YOURSELF

Anyone desiring to join us in living out the way of life described in this rule of life may do so privately by adopting any or all of it to their own life.

For those wishing to make public their commitment to adopting this Way for their lives, we invite you to notify us of your intention via thetrinitymission.org so that we might pray for you on your journey. You will also find there the resources discussed in this book and many other aids to assist you in living out this Way.

And finally, anyone who wishes to formally adopt this rule of life and to have the benefit of guidance and fellowship in living it out may apply to our Oblate formation program at thetrinitymission.org.

May we all abound more and more in love as we grow in the grace and knowledge of Jesus Christ. To Him be all glory, honor, and praise. Amen.

CREATING A RULE FOR YOURSELF AND YOUR FAMILY

Initial Thoughts on Your Rule

WHAT IS A RULE OF LIFE AND WHY SHOULD I HAVE ONE?

A Rule of Life is simply a well thought out, general description of how you want to live your life to the glory of Jesus Christ. The reality of our lives is that we live our day-to-day intending to start this thing next week - do that thing when we get through this busy season - put our money there when we have a little more of a safety-net built up.

The point of having this section to our Rule of Life is to take some time to think through real-life things now, to think through our own gifting and calling, and then to chart a course onward and upward into the knowledge and experience of God's grace, to describe what we want our life to look like and to describe it realistically.

This will take some honesty and humility. *The Way of Christ* is not a calendar or an agenda. It is a standard that you can use to measure (like a "ruler") whether or not you are becoming the person you believe that Christ has made you to be.

Furthermore, this personalized section of the Rule is not ironclad. It should be reassessed at least yearly. As your life changes and as you mature in Christ, your path forward will likely change as well.

May God bless you in this endeavor.

SUGGESTIONS FOR THE PROCESS OF MAKING THIS SECTION OF YOUR RULE

As I said earlier, a Rule of Life is to be a well thought out description of your life. For this reason, I'd suggest prayer and some sort of fasting to open yourself to the Holy Spirit's guidance before you begin developing your personal section of the Rule. If you are able, you may even want to go off for a quiet personal retreat to work on this.

After you have developed a draft, show it to people who know you well and are willing and able to shoot you straight. A Rule of Life is to be reasonable, but it is also a spiritual discipline. A Rule that subtly encourages greed or slothfulness (for example) may be reasonable but it's not really what we're trying to achieve.

After you have made your personal section of the Rule, print it out. You might even give it to a couple trusted friends and explain to them that this is the sort of person you want to be and ask if they would be willing to ask you about it every now and then.

As you can probably already imagine this is not an easy thing to do. It's a whole lot easier just to imagine yourself developing good habits and disciplines than it is to write out those habits and disciplines and show them to someone else as goals you wish to achieve.

As a last thought before we begin making your personal section, it should be pointed out that everyone's structure will be different. Some people are "check-box" people and they want to have a list of things to check off. Perhaps things you do each day, other things you do each week, each month, etc. Their Rule will maybe look a little more like a list of things to be done at particular frequencies.

Other folks are "trajectory" types. They want to have a general mission and vision described but for them the check-boxes begins to feel legalistic and confining. Their Rule may be a more general description of who they believe they are in Christ and where they want to go with that.

The important things for either type, and all types in between, is that your Rule is Observable, Measurable, & Attainable.

Observable – others can see whether or not you are living up to your Rule.

Measurable – it can be determined whether or not you are actually living up to your Rule.

Attainable – your Rule is realistic for who you are and where you are in life.

WHAT SORTS OF THINGS SHOULD YOU HAVE IN YOUR RULE

Now let's think through some of the things you should consider having in your Rule. Because we are uniquely called and gifted, everyone's personal section of the Rule will be different. But in case you are reading this without the advantage of assistance from a spiritual director, I want to talk though some of these things in a little more detail and offer what I believe are helpful standards to set for yourself.

• EUCHARIST ATTENDANCE

Gathering together as the Body of Christ, worshiping Him in a manner consistent with His people's worship throughout history, and receiving His Body and Blood so that He may dwell in us and we in Him as we go out into the world to be salt and light, to be Christ Himself among a crooked and depraved generation – this is the backbone of the Christian life. It should be the backbone of our Rule as well.

The early church believed this so strongly that there was a time that missing the Eucharistic worship 3 times in a row resulted in ex-communication. Certainly, our own ideal should be to participate in the Church's worship and communion on every Sunday. If this is not possible because of health or geography, then, as we have already discussed in the common section of the Rule, you will have to adjust accordingly.

• DAILY PRAYER

There was a time when it was not unreasonable for the Church to gather together physically every day for the Daily Office. Perhaps (and sadly so) it may not be possible to do this in our modern lives.

However, praying the Offices at home or joining in with our Audio Daily Office podcasts at thetrinitymission.org are good ways to continue this practice even in the modern era.

You may want to write out your reasonable expectations of yourself regarding a habit of daily prayer. If this is a new step for you, then you may find that our resource *Getting Started with the Daily Office in the Household: a Prayer Guide for Individuals and Families* may be a helpful tool.

For those who have families, praying these services at home will probably have some cross-over with the next section – Family Prayer and Scripture Reading.

• FAMILY PRAYER AND SCRIPTURE READING

Whether you are newly-weds, empty-nesters, a single parent, or a couple raising children together it is crucial to the formation of the family as a whole as well as the individual members of it that you pray together (for this purpose "prayer" includes listening to Scripture, praying pre-written liturgical prayers, and free-form prayers).

How often you pray together and at what time will be different for every family but there should be some sort of rhythm where your family knows it will gather for prayer.

For the parents who feel a little uncomfortable starting this sort of thing we have the book: *Getting Started with the Daily Office in the Household: a Prayer Guide for Individuals and Families* at thetrinitymission.org. We are working on other resources for you as well so keep checking in.

• PERSONAL PRAYER & SCRIPTURE READING

The book just mentioned is also helpful for this part of your daily life (and it should be daily). It should also include the things I mentioned above concerning prayer (i.e reading Scripture, praying pre-written liturgical prayers, and free-form prayers).

• PERSONAL STUDY

We are all called to be continually growing in grace but not everyone is called to greater academic attainment. You *may* want to have as a part of your Rule some expected frequency of reading Christian writers, listening to podcasts, etc. Some amount of this is usually good but it's not for everyone. I mention it here to stress the point that it is not the same as Personal Prayer & Scripture Reading.

• SPIRITUAL DIRECTOR

If you don't have one, now is a good time to think about getting one.

• MEALS WITH CHURCH

Where we have our meals, how we have our meals, and with whom we have our meals says a tremendous amount about our priorities and even our theology.

We'll suffice it to say that there should be some frequency to your sharing a meal with people from your church. This does not mean the whole congregation (though that should occur too) nor does it mean that it must be the same people every time, in fact, it probably shouldn't be.

• FAMILY MEALS

By a family meal I mean any meal that occurs in your home (or a picnic or something) and includes all of your family (though others may be present as well). The family meal is perhaps one of the primary ways that a family establishes its identity (the relationship of this discussion to the Eucharist is not incidental).

In our modern lives a family meal can be excruciatingly difficult to schedule, but I'd challenge you to seek to make it the norm rather than the exception. That is to say that at least one meal is had together on at least 4 days of the week.

• FASTING

So enough about all this eating, what about not eating? We have given a general fasting regimen in the Rule. How will you apply it to your life?

• SOLITUDE / REFLECTION / PERSONAL RETREAT

This might be the one quality that all the saints of the Church's history have had in common. What will be your own standard for yourself each year?

• BUDGET: SPENDING / GIVING / SAVING

When is enough enough? Many of us will continue to earn money until we pay the undertaker, and that's usually a good thing.

But there is probably a point in all of our lives where saving becomes idolatry and is motivated by greed or fear. Likewise, left unchecked our spending often becomes fueled by fear, envy, lust, or gluttony. Where is that point for you? You might give it a real number – as in, when I have $xx in savings, I will begin giving at an even higher level. If you don't give it a number now, that point will always be: just a little bit more.

You can always change the number later on. But when you do, you'll be aware that you are making a change and therefore the change itself will be intentional rather than accidental.

• ISAIAH 58
Read it. Then read Isaiah 1, Isaiah 61, and Matthew 25. Then think about what specific things your Rule should include along these lines.

• PERSONAL MISSION STATEMENT / FAMILY MISSION STATEMENT
For some of you, this may be the primary element of the personal section of your Rule. Just like for an organization, a personal mission statement is clear and generally describes the sorts of things you are about. Also, like in a corporation, a mission statement helps you to decide what things you will not be about. A mission statement can be a very handy companion to the budget section above.

• SERVICE IN COMMUNITY
This is different than the Isaiah 58 section above. This would include more general types of service (i.e. a youth group leader, a community gardener, a mentor, or some other sort of work that benefits your local community).

• MARRIAGE
Time away together and alone? Dates? Marriage enrichment workshops? What are your goals and plans to achieve them?

• HEALTH & PHYSICAL FITNESS

As you make health and physical fitness goals remember that the Rule should describe who you are generally not detail out your week.

• CONSUMPTION

We live in a world that tries to make us more and more consumers of products and less and less creators or producers. What would it look like in your life to limit consumption (spending, eating out, buying things you could easily make yourself).

An activity as simple as learning to make butter from milk or to make bread from scratch can begin to change our whole outlook on such things.

• MEDIA

Take a minute to add up the hours you spent on social media this week (and then double it to get the actual number you probably spent). Add to this the hours watching TV or movies or surfing the internet. These things perhaps are not intrinsically bad. But your Rule is a good way to intentionally determine just how much of your life they will take up.

By the way, did you know that the word "muse" has to do with being thoughtful or being creatively inspired. Thus, the word "amuse" means not being thoughtful or creatively inspired.

What are the differences between "a-musement" and "re-creation?" How can your Rule direct you toward the one and away from the other?

EXAMPLE
PERSONAL
SECTIONS
OF THE RULE

Following are some examples of the personalized section of our Rule of Life. Yours will most likely look very different. The important thing is that it is observable, measurable, and attainable.

John Doe
The Way of Christ
My Personalized Details

General Statement:

I am a child of God, a husband, a father, and a creative person desiring to use business as a form of mission in my community. In all aspects of the way that I love my wife, lead my family, serve my Church and community, and conduct my business(es) I will seek to bring glory to Jesus in my thinking, my speaking, and my actions. Furthermore, I recognize that my family, my church, as well as the families of my employees can be blessed or hurt depending on my obedience to this manner of life I am describing.

By the grace of God and the enabling of the Holy Spirit, this is what my life will look like:

Personal

• time in prayer and Scripture
    [Ideal: daily – Acceptable: 5xweek]
• extended quiet time (practicing solitude)
    [Ideal: weekly – Acceptable: 2xmonth]
• fasting
    [Ideal: Wed & Fri until 3pm – Acceptable: weekly]
• Matthew 25/ Isaiah 61 etc. activities
    [Ideal: weekly – Acceptable: monthly]
• quiet retreat
    [Ideal: quarterly – Acceptable: yearly]
• meet with a spiritual director
    [Ideal: monthly – Acceptable: quarterly]

<u>Family</u>
- family meals [Ideal: daily – Acceptable: 4xweek]
- family prayer [Ideal: daily – Acceptable: 4xweek]
- special activity with (wife) only
    [Ideal: weekly – Acceptable: monthly]
- special activity with (child) only
    [Ideal: weekly – Acceptable: monthly]
- play-time with (child)
    [Ideal: few minutes daily – Acceptable: 4xweek]
- special family events
    [Ideal: weekly – Acceptable: 2xmonth]

<u>Church</u>
- Eucharist/worship
    [Ideal: weekly – Acceptable: 3xmonth]
- Daily Office (at home, may include above prayer times)
    [Ideal: 2xday – Acceptable: 5xweek]
- Daily Office (gathered together)
    [Ideal: weekly+ – Acceptable: 2xmonthly]
- Service to my Church
    [Ideal: 2xmonth – Acceptable: monthly]
- Other forms of service in the local community (may include Matt. 25 above)
    [Ideal: 2xmonth – Acceptable: monthly]

<u>Finances</u>
- As a family to live on $x or less annually (including all savings, vacation, etc.)
- To give 10% of annual amount (above) to Church
- To give/spend 50% of amount in excess of $x each year to works for God's kingdom with emphasis on justice and mercy causes/ministries

- When total value of all savings/assets > $xx, then we will give 75% of amount in excess of $x/year to works of God's kingdom

Business

- To pay well above the average for employees who have demon-strated loyalty
- To have at least x employee(s) who may not have an opportunity to work elsewhere (prison record, foster kid, etc)
- To know the names of my employees spouses (and children??)
- To determine creative ways to have my employees celebrate the Holy Days that I celebrate (e.g. treats, bonuses, parties, etc)
- To be known by my employees as both hard-working and compas-sionate
- To be known by peers as fair and of the highest integrity

Jane Doe

A Design for My Life
(my personalized section for living The Way of Christ)

I am a child of God, a wife, a mother, a daughter, and a teacher. I want to love my husband excellently and be an exceptional mom. I want to raise up my children as well as my students to be strong and independent men and women who know, love, and serve Jesus Christ as their King.

Weekly Eucharist/ Worship

Prayer & Study
Monthly: Read a sermon or
letter from the early Church
Weekly: pray with Women's group
Daily: Prayer & Scripture

Disciplines
Yearly: personal quiet retreat
Monthly: meet with spiritual director
Weekly: fast
Daily: 20 minutes listening prayer

Wife
Yearly: Marriage Retreat
Monthly: Date Night
Weekly: Buy or make
something special just for John
Daily: pray for him

Mom

Yearly: weekend trip with each kid alone
Monthly: special activity with each
Weekly: fun family activity
Daily: make healthy meals,
tell them I love you at least 10x each,
pray for them each

Other

Yearly: help run summer program for special needs kids
Monthly: have someone to dinner that we don't know too well
Weekly: serve at the shelter
Weekly: help kids Skype with grandparents
Daily: speak kind words to a stranger

John Doe, Jr.
Rule of Life – the particulars

My General Mission

God has made me creative, caring, and steadfast. It is my desire to serve Him in my personal and professional life by cultivating the Kingdom of God in those around me; by caring well for everyone who He puts in my path; and for exemplifying steadfastness, integrity, and reliability at work, with my church, and among my friends and family.

Regular Practices I want to Keep

Daily:
- Daily Office at home
- 10+ minutes reflection on Scriptures
- Keep prayer journal
- Engage someone in meaningful conversation (that they are interested in)
- Intentionally speak kindly to 10 people

Weekly:
- Sunday Worship
- Serve Tue & Thurs at the foster home
- Wednesday Evening Prayer & dinner at the church
- Exercise 30minutes – twice
- Creative writing 1hr – twice

Monthly:
- Meet with spiritual director
- Have people over for dinner party
- Have a quiet retreat
- Develop main hobbies (birding, beer & wine making, bread-baking, gardening, cooking)
- Give 10% (on top of tithe to Church) to foster home

<u>Yearly:</u>
- Extended quiet retreat at the monastery
- Learn 2 new hobbies (even if I do not develop them but just so that I can have more topics of connecting with others)

Audio Daily Office – a podcast of the daily office. Also available on iTunes or any other podcasting app.

Getting Started with the Daily Office in the Household – a guide and prayer-book for those who are just beginning to pray formally in their household. It contains a section focused specifically on praying with children.

Sacred Stories of the Old & New Testament – the child appropriate, narrative portions of the ESV Bible presented as a "chapter book." Especially helpful to use for the readings at family prayer times with children.

Making a Good Confession – a guide for an extensive examination of our lives in preparation for confession. It includes a step-by-step of what to expect if you have never practiced confessing to a priest/presbyter before.

And various other podcasts, videos, blogs, and book recommendations.

The Way of Christ: an interpretation of the Rule of St. Benedict for people with jobs and families in the modern world, Copyright ©
2021-2022 by Michael Thorne Jarrett

thetrinitymission.org

ISBN 979-8-9854410-7-9 paperback

Made in the USA
Monee, IL
10 January 2023

24970503R00038